Diaspora³

Andrew Geoffrey Kwabena Moss

First Published: 2023

10 9 8 7 6 5 4 3 2 1

ISBN 978-0-6454326-3-3

Printed & Bound in Australia

Published by RoseyRavelston Books

roseyravelstonbooks.com

For Oscar, Charlie & Ruby

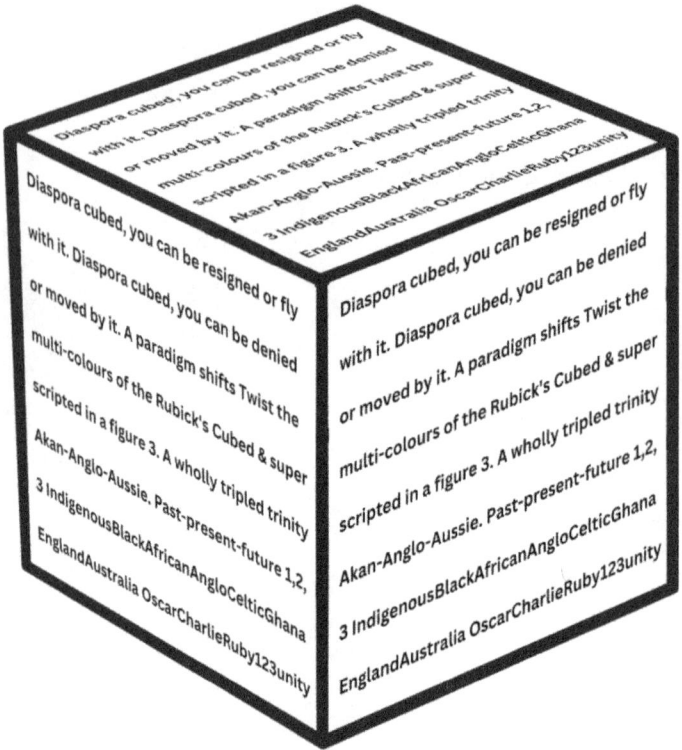

Diaspora: the dispersion or spread of any people from their original homeland

Cube: (noun) a symmetrical 3d shape – either solid or hollow (contained by a net of 6 equal squares)

(noun) Maths – a product of a number multiplied by its square, represented by a superscript figure 3

(verb) 1. raise (a number or value) to its cube

2. cut into small cubes

PART ONE
Past - Present
- Length - x

A Global History
An Ecology of Healing
Black Caesarean
Transportation Evades
John Randall
Underclothed
Genetic Threads

A Personal History
North-West Diasporas
Friday Night at the Corrib
Parallels, Longitudes & Latitudes
Forbes Far From Normal
Hog Hunter Dave
At the Races
Yamala's Didges
Sitting at the Edge of Roebuck Bay
Cable Beach Calypso

Then on Arrival
Double Diaspora (Home)[2]
Remote Control Culture Shock
The Australian Nightmare
South Coast Laurie

PART TWO
Present - Breadth
(Of Experience) - x

Place peoples Place
Brighton-Le-Sands of Time Shift
Under a Purple Bowral Sky
Rugby Gala(h) Day
Bangalow Cowboy
Apex Gangland Myths
Canberra Fortunes Chances
Danni Girl & Danny Boy
Skipper at the Bowlo
Sausage Sizzle & Pink Lobster Sonnet
Six o'clock Pigs Swill

Nature of Places
More Wildlife
Run
Won't You Smell the Roses
Olympic Rings
Rocky Hill Webs
The Escarpment Carnival
Benedictions

Familiar/ Personal/ Family
Thirteen Year Sentence
Drifting CitiXen, Drifting DeniZen
Epithalamium
Green Eyes in a Stormy Night
Antipodean Dream
Great Barrier Belief

PART THREE
Present - Future
- Height -

Peoples place Peoples
Pt I – Naming Ceremony
Pt II – Without Ceremony
Mined & Yours
Smart Televisual Reflections

Places of Nature
Revolutionary Still Life
Migratory
Wetlands Reverie
Scar(r)ed Seed
After the Flood
Healing Tree

Family/ Personal/ Familiar
Watch 'em Grow
Uncle & Son
Soccer Star Floodlights Clouds
Cupid's Vinculum
Identity Whispers
New Australian Wave
Peace After Pain
Diaspora[3]

PART ONE

Past - Present - Length - x

A

Global

History

An Ecology of Healing

Anthropocene defeating
Indigenous nations rise, back up
Barren lands reinitiate
Nullifying terra nullius, nutritious firestick reignition
Ancient agricultural systems recognition
Magical ecological intuitions rekindled

Planetary business rebalancing scales
Rainbow Snake swallowing bolung,
regurgitating Earth with water
Dry to wet, head to tail fertilisation of saline soil
Re-coralising barriered sadness
On the boundaries of civilisation

Reharmonising, resynchronising moon tides
In time with ecological rhythms
Rebirth from ancestral womb
Blood-life source, cosmic strength inner force:
Rains fall, seasons change, animals multiply
To the power of infinitesimal cyclical renewal

When ecology is at risk
Karadjeri let blood flow red
Fertilising parrot fish
Brings success in hunting, gathering
Observance of own-kill rules
Ensuring plentiful supplies of food
Myth ritual totemism inseparable unity principle
Collective symbolic actions realised

To find answers, we return to a place before the beginning
In our minds moving forth back in time ceremony:
gamil-bidiwii epistemology
Healing scarred tree pedagogy
Kamilaroi stories of preservation
passed down to cultural custodians
generation to generation
Memic immortality seen, heard in the rippling rings of trees
Carved stories, documents, charted time immemorial dreams
Ancient symbols sing and dance: Kubbaanjhaan
Bloodlines flow through landscapes sustaining life

We chant as we carve,
One ochered body, entranced
Reciting stories, protecting
Opening the genetic memory of responsibility
Collective consciousness, recreation of DNA's
double-helix umbilical cords
pulling mind's heart connecting Country
Carved stories, sharpened tools honed on whetstone earth
Moving forth back Dreaming: Burruguu-ngayi-li
An ecology of healing
Anthropocene defeating.

Black Caesarean

I am sorry to say, that I need to remove it,
surgically, burst your bubble
This amniotic sac of trouble
Clinically I'll sterilise the archives
I'll dig and scrape for facts
And draw neat narrative lines
with the scalpel, poised for precision

For your own good I'll split your history
Veins, raw nerves and tissues of lies
By C-section inside and deliver the naked truth
I'll drain the fluid membrane fabrication
Rupture its protective front foot defence
Somersaulting confidence

History's womb must be laid open
Roll open the tombs of saviour
Let's break its waters in diluvial denouement
Pour libation, celebrate the wetting of the head
and rituals, a Biblical cutting of an umbilical cord
that feeds misinformation,
read at the very placenta, propaganda
I'll deliver you a black baby son or daughter
Founder of your Nation

My first delivery is an African, proud
From a line of marronage
Traced back from West Africa to Jamaica
To the States, Britain then to Australia
Here in Australia, Black Caesar!
What a revelation, unwritten in textbook pages
A Loyalist runaway slave who fought with the British,
ingratiated by their promises of manumission

in the American Revolution, at the birth of its Nation
In the early days of settlement
Dependable, Caesar was regarded with favour, a strong
labourer
None were of greater stature, a giant of a man
Alas his appetite could not be satisfied
A rationed allocation that took no account of his size
After ten hours of backbreaking labour each day
He stole to get enough to eat

Caesar was caught and sent to Garden Island imprisonment
The maroon in his blood coursed in his veins, he did it again
He took a boat and rations and went off into the bush
Australia's first bushranger, following
Maroon traditions of survival against oppressors
So, you see just like Nanny in Jamaica
It's not the story White Australia favours

Cutting through the interior of dense forests,
corridors of obfuscation hacked
with his cutlass blade making incisions,
a C-section through History

The messy afterbirth of a colonial nation
High time we delivered
a Black Caesarean to Australia.

Transportation Invades

January 20th, 1788

The surgeon lifts the hinges, the hatches
secreting ship bilge, risen high on cabin panelling
it tarnishes the silver officers' buttons black,
John Caesar is on board, inhaling noxious gas,
In salty sickly waves, food waste, stale
water, excrement, noxious effluvia, vomit wafts

Convict teeth loosen in jaws as muscles pulp
Scurvied skin bruises at a touch, fragile bones
Cannot support, proud warriors skin adorned
in ivory bone jewels, through noses,
right front teeth remove, directing a small pale man
in ill-fitting red uniform to match his face
to a fire stream, unassuming of his invasion

First Australians watch a man of similar hue
Different from the ghosts, still haunting
Nevertheless, an alien, dressed in bizarre costume

Vainly the Scarborough working party cut coarse long grass,
the prehistoric sprawl of megaflora lying on the forest floor
In the hope of creating, a last outpost of empire's sentinel

Blackened sand soil holds Jurassic tree trunks, rise
Fifty feet high, contorted limbs stretch in sky
Remorseless sun beats down on his darkened brow
Shade slivers weep narrow gum leaves, straggle
light in sea breeze, soft timber breaks, low boggy
mosquitoes dance, their fiery humming fuselages
buzz in tawny taut skinned tepid water

Forced, interlopers clutch at strange weapons like teddies
move north to Sydney Cove, a settlement ready
made for flagstaff hoisted Union Jack, accompanied by
fireworks
flex iron muscles to annotate arrival
Volleys puncture humid air, red, white and blue plumes
flutter above, the Governor at sunset steps ashore
June 26th, 1788, invading in the name of King George

John Randall

A six-foot black man towering, rising
in bright yellow uniform, shining
leader of the New South Wales Corps drums
up a band of brothers in a Rum Rebellion

John at the vanguard of four hundred armed
Redcoats in rowdy procession readying,
along Bridge Street to Government House
they assemble to arrest William Bligh
hiding behind his bed for his crimes

John was a military man with steady aim,
he sprang with agility to fortune and fame
'roo shooting, the Governor's game-
keeper, supplier of meat for the early settlers

A talent at the flute and tambour
John joined the Corps as a drummer
Blowing his pipe and beating a skin
Strong in broken places, hidden within

Evacuated to England in 1783
a closely ironed felon of the 63rd Regiment,
demobilized and demoralised, immediately
found guilty of stealing a silver watch chain,
The clock stopped, sentenced to a Manchester jail

Facing transportation on the Ceres to Africa
to Lemain Island, his conviction passage
for 'desperate and dangerous disposition'
to rot and remain for the rest of his days

Parliament was persuaded of the ill state
of safety and hygiene on that island preyed
After investigation the African Solution lay
abandoned, until Matra, Loyal New Yorker,
midshipman on Cook's discovery voyage
promulgated another destination,

an impossibly remote place
Isolated, thirteen thousand miles away,
on the coast of the southern continent,
to Botany Bay, John sailed despondent

Yesterday I played the video of a colonial past
In History Period 3 for my class,
We dimmed the lights and watched in the dark
None of us saw John Randall leading the march.

Underclothed

Old Fan wore gloves and long sleeves
Long skirts in the summer heat, she covered up
Her sable skin was eyed suspiciously for being Indigenous
Old Fan's dark fears covered up her darker skin
Her black convict history, kept under wraps, within
A shameful secret

Behind closed cupped hands, families whispered
Murmurs beyond closed doors, to save public face
family lore put forward other stories, of free settlers
clothed in extravagant propaganda,
dressed up in assimilation

Old Fan had plenty to be proud about
She, a granddaughter of Black Founders
on the First Fleet, Martin and Randall
Two men who shaped the nation, erased
by White Australia's policy, its annals of amnesia
Faces that didn't quite fit,
the mythic narrative.

Genetic Threads

For William Cuffay

Cuffay's granules sprinkled across a sea,
a spume of milky white colonial dreams
surplice cottas and cassock black rocks crash
Stir, golden brown whirlpools pull Atlantic back
to the Pacific, the Americas to Africa,
Europe to Australia, mainland to Bass Strait

William threads genetic memories
in double stitched helix DNA
Deformed, defamed yet surviving tailor made
as we listen to the whisper form a choral
roar rich and poor in injustice, roar
stitched across time and space, in troughs and waves

breaking free of triangular enslavement
the yoke, cracks under his imagination
A sailor following a six-point charter
Stars shine across the furrowed oceans
Illuminating paths from Africa
to America, Britain to Tasmania.

A

Personal

History

North-West Diasporas

Biltong, boardies, Billabong and Tim Tams
Bagged, tagged and entangled Antipodean Man's travels
At the Oz shop next to the Polski sklep,
the delicatessen opposite the Czech
knocking shop, down the High Road, along
from Willesden and Dollis Hill brothels
                                        Join the throng

The disillusioned diaspora squash and spill
their plastic chalices of cider and black
At the pews of The Church around electric
campfires, gazing up at The Outback
At the Southern Cross cornered, by a Union Jack
Moored on an odyssey through wine dark seas

As the pints get d(r)owned, ocker accents flounder
Inflections rise in uncertain intonation
The metal container of TNT
magazines, Metro blast roadside detonation
Spin Katherine wheels lighting up explosive dreams
White hot fuses glowing magnesium

Atop Willesden Green's terraces sausages sizzle
on square plates next to oil drummed sliced jerk chicken
Matildas waltz on the balcony to calypso rhythms
Boxing gloved kangaroos caught limboing in a ring
with Haile Selassie riding, a lion of Judah
Brondesbury Park lined with churches, synagogues,
mosques, Baptist chapels and temples to Buddha

The silver fern Kiwi plumbing van teeters
on double yellows by the One Stop Shop
Parked cars dangle beaded with rosaries
and immigrants' sweat, Om calligraphy,
Sikh daggers, Afro-Caribbean red,
gold and green triangular pennants and flags'
tassels sway hosannas away from hassles
wave on turquoise seas, buoyant
on white sandy palm fringed beaches

As an Akan brother in a Willesden library
traces his lineage through Egyptian valleys
Of Kings, sun beating on his neck
He flywhisks with the tail of an elephant
hopes and dreams carried on gold palanquins
Avoiding the troughs, history's disappointment

Aussies board pillar box red double deckers
to Ascot, through market towns and villages
Where their stories started, sails on the First Fleet
convicts tethered to dissidents and free settlers

Two halves of the same story
On NW2 & 6 borders
Diaspora seeds, sons and daughters
scattered by winds of change
We peck the ground for clues and decorum,
                              questioning 'normal'?

Saffa skateboarders roll bespoke bathtubs
enamelled and clawed feet flip flop in exposure
Bob along the cobbled streets of Lonsdale, muse
at Mursi and Maasai elongated ear lobes, listen
to stretched stories of Kiwis at the weekends
Comin' in from the cold, tube fuselage
opening their beaks doing pelicans
Swallow and regurgitate vomit bombs

Laughing at the gravity of beer bongs
in a land pronouncing flip flops over thongs,
corner shops over dairies
'May as well make the most of it,'
they say, 'we won't be here for too long.'
Squashing vowels, digraphs and diphthongs
Cherishing dual nationality passports

Not quite the hardship of wind rushed middle passages
dancing and floating bronzed leaves float in breeze
the autumnal airs and graces of Gladstone Park
Passing London on a hydrofoil jet stream
On high E wave rush and booze Contiki
Troy and Kel's odyssey to Santorini

Two halves of the same story
On NW2 & 6 borders
Diaspora seeds sons and daughters,
scattered by winds of change
We peck the ground for clues and decorum,
No need to question two sides
                              Of the same story.

Friday Night at the Corrib

After a week teaching down the pit
and up the flights of stairs in a Victorian red bricked
workhouse in five, 9 to 3 shifts, trying

to mine for aha moments
at the fraying seams of blackened boards'
chalk and talk faces opposite me
we, the Antipodeans and I decide to treat ourselves
across the road at The Corrib Rest, for a few

Dick Whittington and wizards from NZ and Oz
on a pilgrimage for black gold at all costs
We sip our Guinness reverently, obsidian encased
chalices in bevelled edge pint glasses followed by shots
fired on the other side of Kensal Rise
and debrief incidents during the week, crack mums
and alcohol foetal kids assuming positions inherited

Amidst the ceilidh din of kith and kin
Riverdance sprays, spits its rain against the window
Drips in zig zag rivulets
Tin whistles and bodhran beat in time and quicken
tap our fingers, girls above in sequined outfits
to the rhythm, dance
in Alice's Wonderland House of Cards
As we drown yesterday and tomorrow's sorrows

We sip and slur our words until
it becomes a blur.

Parallels, Longitudes, Latitudes & Latrines

Bursting and busting
Parallels, longitudes and latitudes
Six invisible degrees of separation mapped
Rimes the immigrant mariner travelling
Albatross around neck,
Fleeting dreams carried on Atlas's back
The street signs read
like spoilt A-level History papers
ripped text waves ripple colonial textbook pages

Flicking through six invisible degrees
of separation
Pitt, Elizabeth & Castlereagh
streets we weave,
parallels, longitudes and latitudes

Another Hyde Park spreads
its bold new world buttress, roots
me to unfamiliar yet familiar soil

At the station, the same Victorian tiling joins
each grouted piece vanishing points and voids
Yet, in this new world room is made
Underground, toilets are available
I relieve myself in this
familiar yet unfamiliar nation

Forbes Far From Normal

Bullock cart streets twice as wide as London yawn
Lattice patterns elaborate messages in Forbes

Adorned terraced country town palaces
Imagine convicts, bushrangers and ballads

Mail coach hold-ups boast at Eugowra
Out skirting, you pass sixties blonde brick

Ben Hall Motor Inn stagnant pool images
Rendered in peeling paint green and cream

The sign quips tourists, there'll be no robberies within
The rising intonation of a nation instated larrikin

Clean comfort affords accommodation
The neon announces its vacancy

And in that split second the front bar hushes
like the forked tongue of spaghetti western cusses

Saloon doors bat their eyelash jalousies
In jealousy's disapproval stetsons cock back

Here there's only room for blackfella abeyance
The neon wire suspends it's no vacancy message

Hog Hunter Dave

Dave, a furry red headed huntsman, paces
Burnished skin clinging to Hard Yakka cotton twill
A khaki cowboy; a stockman
Ranger shirt and stubby pants hoisted high
like an NRL footballer on Friday night
Dave plays the conversational ball
disrupting ruck's rut and lull, we listen enthralled
His belt boa constricting his skin-tight pants
Telling tales, spinning yarns how he gallivants
Dave bounds around his Colorbond shed
Nodding up at trophies stag horned with hogsheads
Animated as Rumpelstiltskin circling a campfire
Telling tales, spinning yarns of extinguished desires
The Noonkanbah larrikin laughs
Come morning, Dave hoots to us in his Land Cruiser
A shepherd rounding up Kulkarriya truants

At the Races

Tumblers drunk from fumbled cups of plastic
Mould softly in Broome humidity's grip
by fingertips that balance scales in favour
Refusing to spill a single rum viscous drop
On dusty red orange pindan pavement

Two-up against the wall
"Come in spinner!" twangs the Ringie call
He tosses pennies Sandy Desert bronzed
medallions fly from the jarrah kip, until
it's tossed back in winning to the Ringie

Diggers for national myths lick sugary lips
and gamble on History's prized mate-ship
sink into first fleeting smiles that linger
Heather points to Ernie at the races
Horses, whippets, camels, greyhounds and

greyer nomads in caravans amidst the Dingo
Erect telling amongst wagging tails, of
Chinese dogs, Indonesian sailors,
and Japanese divers. I look for wisdom
Serrated pearls unearthed and etched on faces

Asian-Aboriginal truths whisper
Serrated shells in postcolonial shock
Defensive responses to foreign object-
ions of eons tread in xenophobic legions
on sand, and parasites material inorganic

Lands inside stippled bark terra nullius
in shocking sudden contact with the mantle
Oyster bodies see threatening invasions
Mother Earth, the Rainbow Serpent and father
Yurlungur deposits its nacre

Spreading mother of pearls across the nation
Conchiolin glue holds layers together:
Calcium carbonate, calcite, conchin,
perlucin and mineral aragonite
crystalline, unite in porous clusters

In a shimmery luminous lustre
Through sea embedded sand shifting time
Nacre layers its hourglass to preserve
Building then ridding walled divisions
From the oyster form hybrid new world pearls

as coins spin in the din
and stetsons festooned in cattle tags
tip back in disbelief and sweaty heads scratch
Longhorn insignias stretch on cotton twill
and work shirts, moleskin trousers nibbling
burnished craftsman boots, truths silencing.

Yamala's Didges

Yamala sits cross legged in Broome's Bronx
My mind wonders to NY Projects and a boom box
His wavering voice blows in the hollow
Scarred trees exposed to Stolen Generation sorrow
Didges on kitchen tiling lie discarded, festooned
Stippled lizards, abstract mammals: kangaroos
Yamala speaks softly avoiding eye contact
whilst I try to separate fiction from fact
His wife fills silences with elaborate tales
How his didges fetch thousands at art gallery sales

Sitting at the Edge of Roebuck Bay

Strata of mandala seaside rock
Greet me as I sit at the edge of the dock
Red orange pindan, white sands atop
turquoise sea layers, lead me to dream
as I look out to the turning tides of a clock

To escape the crumbling of Northern Rock,
eroded and rocked by GFC fateful aftershocks
An un-Whittington come to hunt property too late
Alas the mining boom had reduced our luck
to a caravan annexe the bang for our buck,
Larger though than a Kilburn apartment
Perhaps we should have snapped it up
Before prices doubled, plucked up the courage,
avert further financial disaster

Sitting at the edge, I imagined the view
Pearl lugging crews tempted to stay in Broome
Relaxing, unwinding, having a few
Mother of pearls, salt of the earth
I said prayers for them,
midi chalice in hand at the church

Four hundred luggers sent out every day
entering the shallow waters of Roebuck Bay
Local Aboriginal slave labour
Joined in the twenties by Japanese neighbours

Rounded up to dive down the Depths
Shark attacks, drowning, the bends
of ill health, for others to prosper with wealth
Starvation, malaria, malnutrition
Colonial subjects and victims
Adorned with a seaweed Crown of thorns

The privileged grip slippery cutlery handles
and fumble at their pearl buttons of shell
Though the waters soon became depleted
Plans were aboard to head deeper, propelled
by motorised luggers with mechanical pumps

Cyclones and storms and World War One
Broome bombed again, dives grind to a stop
Japanese divers interned
No more mother of pearl
Until they found more at the bay of Kuri
Now I dream of fortunes full circle

Strata of mandala seaside rock
Greet me as I sit at the edge of the dock
Red orange pindan, white sands atop
turquoise sea layers lead me to dream
As I look out to the turning tides of a clock
all is never quite what it seems

Cable Beach Calypso

At Broome in swept a fellow
dread, unbeaten and white bleached
On the crystal treadmill
corrugated sand of Cable Beach
We met, smiling in a mutual decision
Eyes joining dots in facial recognition
Chinese-Jamaican features
mixed with indigenous Taino ancestry
A Calypsonian, from a small island
chain in the Caribbean,
in my palm he pressed his CD
and passed on his melody

Then

On

Arrival

Double Diaspora (Home)[2]

Dedicated to the human Diaspora

<u>Act I</u>

Double helix DNA collides
Double sided consciousness,
double sided survival
Coins, both sides face the colonial toss
and roll of tampered dice

My father went to West Africa,
apart of the British colonial class
His task was to complicate his narrative
not rapacious not pillaging
he married a Kwahu villager
First in her clan, first obibini to marry obroni

Act II

We moved back to the Fatherland
Dad cried tears of sadness for Ghana
tears that lasted
Torn apart a part of two tribes
A family tethered by umbilical cords of DNA and tension
Stretched by the NF in Thatcher's Britain,
to the town and country limits
but an alloy of steely stainless mettle
whose hope did not corrode

I travelled around the world to find a home
A Zion nation wrapped in Rasta Shashemene robes
Japan, the UK then I met an Australian
She traced her family back, from Sydney Cove
to Devon and Burnley, Lancs
To the land of Oz together travelling back
Following a yellow, gold and red brick road
to Aboriginal lands of decimated hope

Double diaspora in helix, back on our travels
Sewing together histories unravel
red, white, yellow, brown and black
Anglo-Ghanaian-Australians
Of a hybrid-hyphen-nation write back.

Remote Controlled Culture Shock

Kath and Kim mince around a suburban block
Blonde brick veneer constructs my culture shock
Shopping malls; fountain gated communities
I can't see the castles from the wattle trees

Colorbond, rabbit-proof pool fences stretch
conquer and divide the Aussie Dream
Enclosing no man's land into territory
Steve flicks next to a documentary

In a larrikin land that I thought was free
of hierarchy, yet I learn of fibro
and Silvertails, Sea Eagles and Rabbitohs
Swooping chips on particle broad shoulders
In disorientation, I'm kept on my toes

All not born equal in the NRL
Is this an Aussie Dream, heaven or hell?

The Australian Nightmare

Alas,
The Australian Dream only got as far
As the manicured lawns that dose in Caringbah
En route we raced and rioted past Cronulla's distressed
Surf and turfed out of the RSL back bar

In God's Own Shire
You hear a muffled exhaust and an immigrant's sigh
Wog Boy numberplates
announce themselves in irony at the traffic lights

Yawning Sylvania Waters
Locked up their bigoted daughters
In reality TV
Screened privately
Moored
By a boater's sea

Saint George's River blood flows cold and indifferently
Artificially, Nightclub chintzy loudspeaker houses
Blast out glam pop into the small hours

The original boat people
Exclude
The other boat people, as there is no room
They ashore us
An I(s)land anchored in the fears of Sylvania's soap opera
Of sons and daughters

In God's Own Country
The Rainbow Serpent is swallowed.

South Coast Laurie

Coasting, Shoalhaven Laurie
Moaned about Lebs, Abos
and Towelheads
Too easy, no worries

He harboured a dislike
of blow-ins
and scabby sou' westerlies

His hobby: barefoot water-skiing
His trade: plastering
Drinking hammer and tongs
Dressed in stubbies, singlet and thongs.

PART TWO

Present - Breadth
(Of Experience) - x

Place

Peoples

Place

Brighton-Le-Sands of Time Shift

Greek mansions gloss obsidian shine
nightclub speakers boom, reveal and seek
Narcissistic nouveau riche reflects hellish
Neo-Aussie Dreams in a Zorba line
along an anodyne boardwalk parallel
to Lebanese cedars and Norfolk pine

The needles stick in migrant paradise
Amidst fifties and sixties Roxy blonde brick,
surf chicks, peroxide and fake orange tiles
Condominiums rescued from Bondi

Long live the hijabs of Brighton-Le-Sands
Pugilists throw silent punches whilst lunching
Cosmopolitan futurists, run fugitives
from rioting Cronulla's surf salutes
Nazi neoprene Hakenkreuz boardies
and Southern Cross faded gun-metal tattoos

To the left and right hookahs bubble
sweet orchard flavours mix apple and crumble
sands at the picnic table, salaam alaikum
drowns out the waves of bovver boots disguised
In Billabong thongs and quicksilver prejudice.

Under a Purple Bowral Sky

Cyclists zoom downhill, cranks and spokes click clack stop-
watch lurid lycra elytra stuck on fluorescent ladybirds' backs
Against a Parker purple inked sky, plastic silver lined clear
and cloudy cartridges about to expire, burst spill and blot
smack the hot tarmacked road, pierced umbrella quilled
nibs raised up expecting paint splosh raindrops, thin rimmed
black elastic bands kiss at the brow, deep brown Nescafé
mixed with Ovaltine, Bowral Brick Federation houses and
churches, chocolate boxed in, between koala chewed
eucalypt, smell redolent spearmint gum leaves evaporate,
curved pieces of masonry cemented together by nougat
mortared memories. Under a purple Bowral sky, look up
to the heavenly, all's not what it seems in my indigo dreams

Rugby Gala(h) Day

Men wearing fleeces with chiselled out features
Turn weather-worn cheeks to cheer on their sons
In the furthest reaches of the Southern Tablelands
On the rugby battlefield there are victories to be won

Enveloped by blue eucalypt amphitheatre
Leagues of gladiators take to their positions
Head-guarded, mouth-guarded,
Body-armoured for fixtures

They speak in sporting codes:
'I'll go five-eighths', 'two passes', 'sixth and last'
Fathers instruct sons in the rules of engagement
On rugby galah day there is no estrangement
Forward passing of culture is never in danger

Boys chase balls
Men chase dreams
Vicarious vultures on the sidelines scream
Galahs peck at holes in defensive formations
On frost bitten grass grind the hopes of generations
Windswept smiles turn to stony grimaces
In the Grand Final Catholic School clash
The score is tied

Coach implores flanker to 'Make a dash…Go wide!'
A perfectly weighted pass answers his prayers
Wing-man arrives to defuse the miraculous missile
A vision flying full throttle over the try line!

Bangalow Cowboy

A psychedelic cowboy rocks and rolls and sits
green gun powdering his cimarron shotgun spliff
Perched on a ladderback and forth
Clint Eastwood on his veranda holds court
Top gun, shields sun with aviator ray bans
Hippy hair hangs limp below a banana brimmed Stetson
cream goanna patterned boot threads etched golden

He rocks back and forth relishing tourist attraction
Front & centre of Bangalow Books swinging his hammock
Teardrops at thin fingers, the cowboy's nails, an ex-
tension of themselves, in tight gloss black
and captain scarlet shellac, onlookers pay homage
to his steer head bolo tie and sparkly jumpsuit,
perfectly executed, jewelled costumes

black crevice metal heavy skull and crossbones
rings lasso his sun speckled knuckles, grip
to the back of the bucking bronco
Bangalow Cowboy sits, shifts on his wooden horse Troy
Cassar-Daley records soundtracks splashing joyous
Northern Rivers and floods, jumping buttresses
roots of Jurassic National Parks, leaves luscious

and lustrous sun stippled canopy crown
Giant ferns and clover quilted forest floors
nestle in megafauna spawning a chorus
of frill necked choristers in rhythmic hypnotic hymn
Cloistered in lush green misericord choir stalls
The Bangalow Cowboy sits aloft at his mahogany pulpit
Preaching to a magical mushrooming audience

Closing his eyes, we join him in prayer
to the faithful, hallucinogenic
Psychoactive worship in ayahuasca churches
Blossoming phosphenes philosophic
The Bangalow Cowboy rides Byron Shire ranges
Suddenly, stands up in twenty-one seconds
gun salutes his crowd, verbal volleys ring

Let off in his sermon, a cacophonous homily
Look at his creation of possibility

Apex Gangland Myths

We hear about Apex Gangs,
lawless youths from South Sudan
Tribal clans discharging firearms
Chicago Bulleted vests holed and red,
Bloods bandanas, back to front caps embed
open wounded harm

But when do we hear of refugee triumphs
Davids lynching Goliaths, rebuilding lives?
Slinging debt to surplus, saving economies
Blossoming labour with innovation, silenced
for the crime of having a different religion
Vigilante violence, wrapped up in a superficial skin

We hear about Apex Gangs,
but what about the Far-Right clowns?
Made up to face and conceal natural layers beneath
Performers mime to distant audiences
Oil based greaseproof opaque
The pratfalls that want to Keep 'Straya White
A continuation of policy, continuing the fight
The Cronulla rioting
Politicians' lips sync boats turned back
Dictation tests disguised by pushing pens inked black

onto paper over cracks erasing,
oral histories and genealogies
of First Australian and Torres Strait Islander nations

Still surviving empowered by genetic memory
DNA strands strong in broken places
Touch the cold hard iceberg tip
Lips pay service to multicultural Australia
living side by side soapy operatic Neighbours,

becoming good friends across the colorbond
Fence Home and Away, sail sunken Endeavours
at subterfuge, the terrorist nullius
Cultural tabular rasa, Dreamtime wiped clean
Eclipsed, by the Australian Dream
By the original boat people, enfeebled.

Canberra Fortunes Chances

Cranskys sizzle

Red wine in plastic is imbibed

Canberra freezes

In midwinter drizzle

Red and white chequered

Croatian past

Canberra FC passes

As the diaspora takes chances

Mensah and Kofi Danning

taming Cooma Tigers

The Croat Ghanaian-Australian team

Advances.

Danni Girl & Danny Boy

For the galvanising of The Galvins

Oh Danny Boy, your puffed out chest, wearing the flushed
cheeks of a robbin' redbreast,
feeding dependents who suckle spare pork ribs in your
welcoming Greenwich Park nest
Perched on a windswept hill with panoramic views 'Galvins
on the Green', galvanising guests
at their Invasion Day barbecue invitation. Facing wide,
baboon pink top to bottom
with a beery glow and a twinkle in the eye. Sun-screened
clouds swirl, circling above
Purple veins join in a reservoir, reflecting sheen joyous
insobriety wide as Lake George

Blundstone boots hi-vis cowboy, builder, shepherd,
concreter, Renaissance Man
butchering sheep at the feast. Catching company in a vice like
grip
Rough palms extend Venus fly trap fingertips. Blood-red
handshakes abound
Cracking irreverent jokes out loud, slapping backs Broad,
ocker accent inflected cheek
by beetroot larrikin jowls. He necks a Coopers Red,
displacing its sediment
A barrel of man with generosity and laughter. Knocking back
bottles; crushing cans
one after the other, after another disaster

Proud of his rich Irish Mancunian stock, exchanges stories
back-to-back
of his Mum's Salford childhood, council flats and eventually
they got her a house

Tipping back, the point of his stetson as the night grows black
Tongues, Aussie, Aboriginal flags
unfurl and relax. An evangelical pastor amongst his flock, holy
matrimony in harmonious baritone,
one man choir, Master Ceremoniously bursting intermittently
into operatic song
of everlasting praise for, 'My bittersweet Danni Girl'

Who dims the lights, bringing home further the night, inviting
the healing of darkness, adjusts
the pitch and tone, turning to Archie Roach at the controls.
Pausing…elliptical
in prayer, to remember how they 'Took the Children Away'.
A story true,
not right, he won't tell lies to you. Bronzed skin, her green
squinting
Bug-eyed, battling eyelids fighting welling tears and imagines.
Her mum, a 'Coota girl'

Once removed for domestic servitude, abused. Ten years
old, her black plaits, undone
chopped off, for two weeks kept below her pillow, crying
herself to forget
She and eight siblings on their way to school. Picked up by
'welfare' officers in a truck and checked
At fourteen sent to farms to wash, cook and clean for the
wealthy
The darker skinned remained to face their fate, Alienated
systematically from their families and
Country. Her grandfather served as a Rat of Tobruk,
honourably discharged and then they took
Took his children away, treated as vermin. Run by Matron
Hiscock's routine military clock
Locked up in 'the morgue' weatherboard building block if
they ran or misbehaved:
Taken away, apprenticed on a conveyor belt of institutional
hell's machinery of dismantling

and separation   Never
ending   anxiety

Nobody said they loved them Nobody cuddled them Nobody praised them

They were told that their parents did not want them
They were told that they did not love them, denied entry at the gates by staff

Passing on inherited trauma, incarcerated sons and daughters' voices

reverberating, Danni hears their calling and looks deeply into the dark
On her cigarette she drags and draws a breath long and hard
A firefly rises phoenix from the ashtray, a lonely light in commemoration.

Skipper at the Bowlo

At the Bowlo the hi-vis skipper steamrolls the seed
at the helm of Empire's virid seas, he grips the steering wheel
Blades submit under cylindrical pummeling steel
Await the nomadic flocks of ageing cockatoos
who descend in threes, race in zimmer framed shock-
absorbed, faster they go splashing gold and green
at the gills, knees and sleeves of shell suits

Old in the dotage of wrinkled skin sheets
onto the baize they peck and parachute
hypnotized by cheese fortune wheels
Living out Crackerjack fantasies
Grey green baize nomads sail sulphur crested
Wave tremulous pensioners frail
Rigid blue rinses hair sprayed graffiti from yesterday
As yesteryear fades a distant memory
Perms and quiffs preserved in aspic haze

Above the mast and rigging
Yellow, black and red flutters in deference
In deferential mistreatment
Misguided by a Southern Cross
a Eureka moment, stockaded in boycott blocked
Stacked against the odds
Where is the mate-ship and democracy?
Cornered by Union cracked Jack fissures
The skipper steamrolls history
Lost and forgotten in pea green seas.

Sausage Sizzle & Pink Lobster Sonnet

Pink lobsters, sausages sizzle in thongs
Meet and two veg, an Abo and a Leb
Feast on a rissole at the RSL
Harmony's rhetoric: everyone belongs
Listen to undercurrents of the throng
Serve policy white privileged heaven rent
Othered sent to Manus for detention
Jettison the national anthemic song

> Whilst at the Bowlo the cheesy wheel spins
> it's black and red roulette for refugees
> trafficked across inhospitable seas
> At the surf'n'turf club above ocean waves
> First boat people's dinghies inflated against sins
> Lifeguards ignore leaky boats in storm haze

Six o'clock Pigs Swill

The six o'clock swill, pigs in shit
swill four X-rated amber liquid
Five o'clock stubble under furrowed brows
Victims Indigenous and convicts now
Blackbirding, First Australians
lured to sugar cane plantations
First Fleeting visitors, swill the amber liquid
All settled around the unlucky horseshoe, victims

Building The Castle in a feudal system
Pigs penned in Animal Farms
Sham democracy sounding alarm
Before the closing bell
down heavenly schooners hatched in hell
Listen to the slurp's death knell
beaded lager froths peals of laughter
Amber opium drunken disaster
Of the masses averting closing time karma

Beer brawling trauma the norm
Step up the urinal brick dais to the altar,
terracotta and black, warriors
wash sorrows, sink, swim and swill
Slam the glass gavel down quick
on the kitchen sink metallic zinc
Crevices etch regret around the horseshoe
Rugged men grip glasses stuck like glue
The landlord surveys damaged waifs and strays
Buttery tiles laid in XXXX tessellation
This is '50s Mackay, Queensland, Aus'traya.

Nature

Of

Places

More Wildlife

I Black and Blue-Tongued Lizard

You shed your blue tongue oily unctuous skin
to suit the continent you're in, chameleon
under morning sun centrally heating
diagonal solar pane zebra crossed scales
in cold blood rushes under a woven mosaic
lies a steely pipework of ventricles and veins
But beneath you bleat black sheep for many
centuries, scapegoated in the ghetto
for usury, ever lending pennies
Yet penned in hope to the tether of your foes.

II Cockatoo Chorus

A giant swarm of iceberg shifts
moving blue, white hornets form
a squawking morning chorus

White paper torn, adorned by crests
wave their sulphurous crowns
Swirl like confetti in a whirlpool drift

A turbulence short-lived
the flock soon lands
and chews on eucalypt

III Cocky Rock

Rocking on guitar string telegraph wire
on an azure sea bob iceberg cockatoos
sulphur crests wave rockabilly hairdos
to god's baton they decorate in colours wash
bottle brushing Il Tricolore glory
as blackfellas on utes sing Dreamtime stories

IV Magpies

A pair of professors eruditely stalk
Dressed in oil slick cassocks

Capped and robed in academic black
Their ermine speckled feathers shine in the sun

Coat tails trailing in deference
They weed out brown wriggly cylinders

Unearthed, slinkies in the dirt
Beaks deep in baize reflection foremost and first

Strutting around my garden quadrangle
Looking to unearth the worms of the world.

V Ibis Landing

The white ibis dot the field, exiled in colonies
Heaven sent by Djehuty, the God of Thoth
The long-nosed jesters probe cathedral green
in masquerade, black shepherds' crooks drop,
possessors of perfect measure,
their featherless heads and necks peck
through aspergillum drizzling weather

a Carr Confoy rugby pitched in muddy puddles
Long seagrass-ward bills fish, hook
for mud camouflaged crustaceans,
in noiseless grace and poise, they teach us
to search for the answers, secrets stuck numb

as my brother's hard-edged words to 'man up'
in woman troubles, replay in my thoughts and bubble
the cauldron hot with despair and failed spells
Ibis, help me change my luck, where to live,
where to love, which country, above and beyond
Ticking time bomb, pendulum of hate and love
estranged, separate and divorced

from Cupid's throbbing, initial choice, help
me execute my flimsy flighty plan
The ibis heart stabbing interrogation persists
whilst extracting moribund morsels with your bill
Teach me perfect timing mastery
at the crossroads, lead me where to go
Along a rickety Blackshaw Track roughly etched
or led up Constable's Harnham path sketched

Question, peck selfish defences, pharaonic ibis
You have travelled across parted wave, red seas
to antipodean Wetlands, from slavery chains

to freedom dreams opening seraphic wings,
stretch and beat ships' canvas sails on green seas
drums in timeless melodies, angels hover
and spread their wings. Let me follow you

Teach trust my inner instinctual bliss
Change weakness into unceasing breath
Swerve and bend your bill to better fortune
Guide me by your silent cooperation,
your perfect sacrifice, at Hermopolis
wrapped contrite in feathered bandages,
ibis mummies, humble my troublesome journey,
Noah release fertility from doubtful drought

VI Snail Trails Blaze

Glide
Translucent movements
Indigenous silver dots
Coruscate the pavement landscape
pioneers in Zion nearing trails
little by little
We shift, shapes like Anansi, blaze
Refugees, cradled
from Ngorongoro Crater's
shellshocked caldera
red hot, ejaculate
belongings
attached on slippery backs

Run

For James Baldwin

And all the time I think of you Jimmy
As my feet chew gravel on bitumen
Blue Heelers baying at the back
A pick-up truck has come
Under the green feeding cockatoos
Brakes and beaks screech
amidst strange fruit leaves

I hang suspended in a land
where the signposts whisper of other times
of Wollondilly, Burbong, Mulwaree,
Tarlo, Burra Burra, Wiradjuri,
Gundungurra, Dharrook, Tharawal,
Lachlan, Pajong, Parramarragoo,
Cookmal and Gnunawal

Yet they write on the wall we are full
They are full of it, we are sick. Red centre pindan
sticks to my stiff bitten upper lip
Scrawled, stuck on rusty Holden ute bumpers
Red necks without frills,
gangrene around the gills without hope
60,000 years but it still isn't home
Blow-ins blown out of all proportion
Sons and daughters locked in prison
Industrial complexes, compounded

Made simple. Navigate the land of Cook
In terra nullius terrorism they took
Where Ned could never be confused
with Billy Blue or Black Caesar stand tall
They seize us, where's the mateship and fair go for all?

Won't You Smell the Roses

Inspired by true events in Goulburn, City of Roses

Proboscises deep in velvet petals
Shane and Sue dip their heads, bees in nectar
reverently smelling,
breathing in the redolence
They tell of local treasure chests
rusty Olympic ringed stories
as old as convict oak
and apostolic gospel glories

Blokes going back to the Duracks
Kings in grass castles,
Queens in honeycomb marvel
Drover cattle travelling
helped by desert Aboriginals

These ladies, my spirit guides are heaven scent
Won't you smell the roses that are left?

Olympic Rings

*For the Sydney 2000 Olympic Rings manufactured
and currently languishing in Goulburn*

Under the torii lintels,
Trucks heave freights laden
on backs loaded with expectation
On either side the cemeteries and jail sigh

A lichen edged and weathered shed
sits next to a crane wearing faded paint
peels to reveal in letters Kermac etched
on its slewing platform in the morning sun

The lower heave and hook
a fishing rod with float that baits
the cerulean sky, a lure to better days
Its lattice boom points an unassuming finger

to Olympic rings, stacked
Sideways drunk in rust
six colours now brown dust and aluminium
A forgotten amphitheatre crowded in optimism

Continents once coruscating
Once bathed in the flame of anticipation
now in the driftwood and flotsam
Jettisoned, snubbed and snuffed

A tumble of vines and cables run-
down, a weedy jungle of lost dreams
Now abandoned in Wasteland mystery.

Rocky Hill Webs

Betwixt the twig's forefinger and index
in its slender tentacles the spider's grip
with tibia and metatarsus lifts
a diamond white encrusted silhouette

Behind Anansi looms, suddenly shapes shift
enshrouded in colloidal silvery mist
Memorial swings sceptre spectre, a stone cold
fingertip vacillates time signatures the metronome
Ephemeral cerement embalms the fluid needle
above, across corroboree tablelands
genetic memories inject the womb

Dreamcatchers tightrope walk the wattle trees
parachute a carapace to prey on, plead
Silken strings, liquid to solid threads lift
in breeze, tales spun in webs from tree to tree
run convection currents carried by rising sun

DNA spirals from inside out
in double helix mystery, threads connect
continents along super tensile land their strengths -
Bridges bring you to your knees, praise be
Onyankopon, for across the seas
on a golden stool palanquin, you've carried me

The Escarpment Carnival

*In celebration of the 59th Annual South Coast Primary
Swimming Championships at Dapto*

Sixties brick veneer juxtapositions jeer and jar
The marble cut Illawarra escarpment
plateau erodes outcropped Anglo-Celtic souls
colonising the ridge with chipped boulders
chain gangs carry the nation's weight on shoulders

The tannoy promulgates swimming heroes
Corrimal East and Narooma battle breaststroke
A bloke in ocker front crawl drawls in slack jaw
presentations freestyled in open mic performance
Pooled battlefields blades cutting backstroke duels
Rubber caps emblazon yellow, green and blue

Sapphire Coast dolphins; Tongorra palm public schools
Vie in abacus float lanes, the minnows swim
Tadpoles spawning strokes amidst kith and kin
Cerulean blue shade sails, bunting and hi-vis
marshalling, heads bob, torsos rise and drop
against currents in a nascent nation gold silver bronzed
by sun, kiosk kissed pindan façade screams
against eucalypt frayed mountainous dreams

Fingers poise buttons swept up in Zorba line
Mosquitoes hover for touches, keepers of time
Parents slap sun screened backs, fetch towels and hats
Slip five-dollar notes in canteen eager hands
Under OZtrail gazebos collect sloppy joes
that boast SSA champs of the South Coast

At carnival they cheer, thonged calves uplift
tense and arise, vicarious jetpilots kiss
their stars, in uproarious strident din
Modern corroborees erase history and sing
Water drowns out, extinguishes the old
Smoke ceremonies' embers smoulder

Coastal casuals in slack jawed national costume
Beach seeking souls jet ski jacuzzi spume
Loose Billabong boardies graze knobbly knees
grey nomad surfers blown off Pacific seas
Concrete slapping quicksilver evading thongs
Skaters gothic robed in jet black Volcom
Vulcanised rubber plim-souls pull up Vans socks
A Nipper's bleached hay tuft scarecrow locks
pokes south of a Santa Cruz canvas snapback

Each Aussie tribal archetype attracts
their own, mesh twinkling magnets in truckie hats
Poolside stroll two lesser spotted country boys
liberated from dusty B&S balls
Swagmen lick chapped lips and swig from the waterhole
John Deere's eyes caught in coastal halogen
headlights, one wears an Endeavour Meats cap
featuring a Merino icon bleating

trussed in RM Williams looking sheepish
Belt buckled, striped shirt rolled up to elbows
boot cut jeans turn up on pointed toes
Leather brown burgundy cowboy boots
effeminate, in adrenaline one rushes to salute
his daughter, 'You're a little legend,' he croaks
rough as a Nullarbor corrugated ode
high praises offered with road base gravel throat
Escarpment lessons invoked in spiritual tones.

Benedictions

Seemingly normal morning benedictions call me
amongst the magpie caw and cockatoo roar
A shimmering breeze flutters its squall
soaking our skin in golden liquid pores
a polished chalice benediction, before
heat reaches, mercury bubbles its cauldron

The un-poisoned chalice brushes our lips
A weathered man from a ute shouts a quip
with a How ya going? exchanges hellos
A flower girl trapped morose in aspic imagination
ignores your wave, remembering bait spurned
Cast out in the playground by othering girls

Cyclists consecrate the wafer-thin pavement
and ring, three warning bells then commend you,
A gentleman stepping aside acolyte
A communion of saints, holy ghosted minds,
Break together the Eucharist bread and wine
Listening keenly for Trinity's chimes...

Familiar

Personal

Family

Thirteen Year Sentence

I travelled thirteen years ago
Transported out of fear
Washed in sepia tones
For home I bled a tear

I travelled thirteen years ago
Like Blackett blown ashore
Blown off course by Cupid's arrow
Inexorably caught

I travelled thirteen years ago
Sentenced by puppy love
In Goulburn's aspic frozen
and torn asunder, numbed

I run around Victoria's Park
Timber fires billow
Corroborees left in the dark
Ceremonies up in smoke

Gothic cathedral dressed emerald
Porphyry catholic stone
The Aboriginals
stranded without a home

Forgotten native history
Before 'first' fleeting narrative
Blanketed Tablelands
Spread settlers' disease/ Extermination planned.

Drifting CitiXen, Drifting DeniZen

Citizen X, Denizen Y
I lost my nationality and I
landed on the floor
The seabed mocked me
An iron anemone once more
Crushed in the watery dusted fist
Serrated edges unfolding
Clam-mooring for my kiss
Unearthing oyster pearly eyes
and lobster lips
Now wrapped up
in a conch's petalled whorl
Lost in a universe
humbled to be small.

Epithalamium

And when you lent me your whiteboard pen
your expression imprinted indelible
Your impression expressed in permanence
Knowingness led to familiarity
A Goulburn girl airlifted on a road trip
From gorillas in misty jungles
Then onto the Greek Islands in the sun

But you hung around to wed me and tell
Pointed messages of Cupid's adventures
Stories of red sandy deserts, spinifex
Echidna quilled love letters and swollen
baobab emotions, opening the valves
and ventricles, opening passages
Untravelled, unmentionable

Now we arrange parenting by SMS
Terse text by poisoned keypad letter
Business-like exchanges from me to you Heather
Do you look back to that Kilburn classroom?
The mosaicked nations we taught at school
Is the whiteboard pen marked indelibly
or erased with ease from your memory?

Green Eyes in a Stormy Night

Leaf clouded mountains cry rain belly clouds

Fingertips of rain drum from bolt upright
Usain's Jamaican lightning & Shango's thunder fight,
Waters break from pregnant clouds' rain bellies tight

Imagine blue tongues under fern frond ponds
In summer's brazier they lay

Oiling daytime mosaic slick scales

Through night green eyes picture infidelities
Projections of my own insecurity

Shake me to morning's core, I awake

I tremor daily to assuage the pain
Crying out, ink spilling its blue tongue tears

pages, awaiting your validation.

Antipodean Dream

When I first came to Australia
It was not the place to go
I'd seen Home & Away and Neighbours
and Young Doctors on the soaps
trapped in an aspic TV screen
But Children of Fire Mountain
were my antipodean dream

Yet I drunk from love's fountain
Soon betrothed to an Aussie girl
two parts of a diaspora
connected two hearts and two worlds
!Flash the Polaroid camera!
Instantly images fading
Saw Kevin's apology
terra nullius evading
Cronulla riots, boardies,
thongs, stubbies, tattooed Southern Cross
gunmetal grey Empire's old
sun wizened Skins and Surfer Boy yobs
Ten-pound poms who remained cold-
shouldering other immigrants

Original boat people
Anglo-Celtic discriminants
dictate tests, jealous, feeble.

Great Barrier Belief

Fifteen years since I met Keith
Fifteen years suspend Great Barrier Belief
Yarns spun of magpie swoops protected by ice cream tubs
From the tropics of Kilburn to Capricorn
Thank you, my friend, for opening the door
The portal to discovering culture
Realising trust and feeling vulnerable

One year sipping a pint on Kilburn High Road
next stop swilling XXXX, a front bar patri-local
Showing me the cane roads, the view from Eimeo
Ghost barks illuminating the mango
tree entrance in photoshopped colours
tropical green and chocolate brown mahogany

The mud crabs, the fibro surf shacks at Seaforth
delivered in self-deprecating drawl
Bunging on the jukebox Aussie Crawl
Kowaha Leaps of faith into unknown pubs
Fearing vests, thongs and lobster no-frills necked troubles

We debate mining, multi-culture,
Blackbirding and Mackay Aboriginals (to name a few)
Home squared to the power of two
We come from diasporas doubled
Forever, your friend, I remain humbled.

PART THREE

Present - Future
- Height -

Peoples

Place

Peoples

Part I – Naming Ceremony

Ceremoniously, I'm named
Kwabena – born on a Tuesday
A name revealing Akan ancestry
You've heard of Kofi Annan surely
Friday born, 7 day names each girl each boy:
Kwasi & Akosua, Kwadwo & Adwoa
Kwabena & Abena, Kwaku & Akua
Yaw & Yaa, Kofi & Afua, Kwame & Ama
Surely, you've heard of Kwame Nkrumah
Leader of decolonial revolution

Kofi, Yaw & Afua sandwiched between
Oscar Thomas, Ruby Jane & Charlie
A hyphen-nation of names:
on a new wave triangular trade
between Africa, Europe & Australia

Twi twiri asin, ho ho ro o nim
I'd sing, fragments from nursery rhymes
Mysterious linguistic lullabies
Wash your face and brush your teeth, I cajoled
Mum to drop the assimilation bomb
of Anglicizing at all costs

light the con-fuse Twi and Mockney molotovs
thrown, Anglo-Ghanaian grenades
thrown from our semi-detached barricade
in language we find our escape
Diaspora language scatters its fragments
Protective shells bursting with bonduc seeds
from Old and New World nickernut grey trees

disperse like oware beads, across
Black Atlantic soils and seas

Explode in culture shock
ejected in brown skin shell trajectory
embedded despite Keep Britain white graffiti
bury the enemy in NF territory

The not quite enunciated Akwaaba
Palavers that arrived on Heathrow tarmac
Crumbs offered at a table of suffering
Maakye Oo' thrown over caste half mornings
Intensified medaase paas without warnings
In yo-yo intonation yo for yes
Daabi for no daabi da for this and that

For you I remove my hat
The mepa wo kyew, I beg you, please

The meda wo ase, thank you,
For you I lay at your feet

The boyish giggles with kwasia obwa
golden cusses ripe as cocoa pods drop from trees
exposing sticky white gooey seeds

In his batakari Dad sang Songs of Ghana Praise
much to childish chagrin and amazement
Intoned yo in elongated tones
a hybrid mix- Wiltshire & Obo

Mum muttered jonsodomi, jonso
when caught short weak at the knees
bursting for the latrine
Private jokes; toilet humour in Twi

Bassa bassa described the troublesome:
the oburoni white man Other, the few
abrofo been-to up-boy Afropeans
at Makola Market bartering, tender as groundnut stew
The Hamburg diaspora branch grown old
Donning MC Hammer pants
billowing silk shirts, adinkra chained gold
Where in Onyame's heaven & earth
were their kente nwetoma robes?

A stolen golden stool reclaimed for me
Medaase papaapa, medaase pii

The pure Twi Mum spoke, as she dialled in
pure phone-ology

London abusua's 'wo hot e sen's?' extended
met with monolingual regret

Now Empire's nomenclature fights back
we regain our Twi Asante prize
History denied, sandwiched on either side
My kids' names:
Oscar Thomas, Charlie
Ruby Jane
Kofi, Yaa & Afua renamed
Anglo-Ghanaian-Australian
rainbow's golden aglow
in a hybrid hyphen-nation
Aba a tena ase
Now that you have come, do stay.

Part II – Without Ceremony

Unceremoniously, I'm renamed
tortured, raped and maimed

Mankind's mother Alkebulan
fruitful Eden denuded, deflowered
Reduced in Phoenician to Africa
Withers in yellowing palm of grand-

mother's hand aboard owari slave boats
Bonduc seeds spread diaspora hopes
Mwari Tendai prayers crammed in holds
sworn under held breath amidst the tempest

Fruit plucked from a basket that floats
Swollen in flowing Nilotic reeds
Part Powell's frothing seas, balm vitriolic speech
Stem the foaming rivers of Tiber's blood
Open red seas, deliver Jah's people from slavery
Hear our prayers, sky god, Onyame up above

We, who cradle civilisation's rifted valleys
trodding lifelong Zion travels, from ocean
to Jochebed middle passages we tread

Until – the rude awakening, Seig Heil!
All hail the merchant ship circling
sails, overblown in the gusts of hubris
Blows the squall, the sea lanes & winds of change
billowing in self-hatred and self-love

Unjust measures teeter the wa(i)vering hull
'free' at the slave traders' coruscating market scales
colonise, unbalanced/ uneasy on Atlantic waves

Carve up, rule, divide the mahogany log,
unaccountable, the ledger for cash,
the roulette helm turns from the red to the black
ahead centuries, before Africa scrambles
from Massa's whip and the lash

Crops: Ivory, Gold and Grain Coasts
Pepper the Atlantic with Slave posts

Dance captives to the Akan drum, walk the plank
climb the greasy crow's nest pole
fly the flag, Union Jack, skull & crossbones
CrammedinAnansilimbo
Question the historical canon
!Explode Elmina detonating hope!

...as greasy palms smear auction block skin
The stench & filth of lucre lubricating
Chained cogs of sinful systems spin
Capoeira moves industrial revolutions
Ambushed by Nanny & the Maroons

Overpowered with plantation tactics
Forever looms, the webs of Anansi
tricksters, house and field niggers
renamed negroes, at home overthrowing

Whom, like Touissant Louverture unite
mulatto, black and émigrés white
& reinstate our names, our nation languages

Once X'd as Brother Malcolm said best
Etched in Detroit Red clay, Cassius to Muhammad
move the mountain, Malcolm to el-Shabazz
Edward to Kamau, Iron Lion Zion

Kush, Punt, Mali; Aksum & Great Zimbabwe
Songhai, Ashanti & Ife; Benin bronze, Kemet & Nok
polished hybrid cosmopolitan culture shocks
Transatlantic, in Bermudan triangular trade
Thrice forgotten but never lost

Unceremoniously, I'm renamed
Rebranded once a slave
From Ghana to England to Australia
Strong in broken places
We will never be erased

Mined & Yours

This is mine as much as yours,
trace crepuscular outlines as they dawn

I tread the Eastgrove ovals of yesterday's massacre
Gandangara elders tell their stories

A chorus formed in many one voice:

These banks are mine as much as yours,
bite the iron, spit the coin

These signs are mine as much as yours,
high on Whiteladies Road
on Blackboy Hill watch Colston
topple
and fall

These slave names mine as much as yours,
a Jefferson, a Washington, a tethered horse

a Detroit Red, a Malcolm X'd to Malik el-Shabbaz,
Mohammad's mountain moulded from Clay

an Arrivant Kamau reborn
This salt and gold are mine as much as yours,
Mansas spread wealth in dusty camel caravan
shifting sands of time

These hourglass dreams are mine as much as yours,
enter REM underwater Drexciyan portals
experimental thoughts

This past is mine as much as yours,
On 21 gun saluting strings, spat in 16 beats

libate our streets, laterite compound soil
in towers blocked, across bedsit endz
in royal palaces repaired by reparations
that will never mend

These words are mine as much as yours,
chained DNA linking ancestors

These beliefs are mine as much as yours,
in kente woven spider tales
Gye Nyame to Anansi and Onyankopon

Smart Televisual Reflections

In that snapped split second I belonged,
we adjusted the television's knob
assembled in a kaleidoscope throng
An oil slick mirror reflecting us
Rainbow nations woven in Benetton
In those minutes our portcullis lifts up
Relieved screw faces loosen and chuckle
At once, all of a sudden Australia's
rosellas resemble a brand-new flag
not the Southern Cross or the Union Jack

But the vermillion earth, the yellow
golden orb, the obsidian black skin
in various red, yellow, brown and pink
across the horizon's continuum
No longer guests on the sofa but actors,
architects of our (own) magical palaces.

Places

Of

Nature

Revolutionary Still Life

The other half bask in the butter cupped sunrise
Trapped in the bowl of the valley's basket
crying out, this is Still Life

as manicured lime lawns sigh,
slope in glacial curve to the kerbside
Above, an ice white cockatoo squawks
its feathered V sign in salute
Sulphur crest bobbing iceberg feathers
on a telegraph wire sending messages

Scarlet jacketed parrots swoop, inky
wings, signalling turncoat livery
Touissant Louverture flies into vision
dressed in revolutionary plumage,
Black Jacobin in blue and red costume
civil war loyalists in ceremonies
bear coats of arms and weapon trophies
Alone, on a green hill with royal palm,
capped in feathered tricorn Liberty
Union fait la force stitched on white ribbon

Two kangaroo statues back-to-back,
frozen, at the bulbous bulge of the cul-de-sac
Mercury rocks at thermometer bottom

Sandstone sentries project palatial delusion
amidst blonde brick veneer revolution
Held hostage in our costly prison traps
Chained to mortgage manacles and shackled
Hardly masking self-satisfied suburban sneer

Cape Cod weatherboard aligns
a perfect horizontal symphony
conducted to Castles free-standing Aussie Dreams
Whilst stymied pawns broke on chequered chessboards
set in flimsy fibro lean to double bricked
Puff their timber fired chimneys in indignation
heritage listed proudly, first fleeting surveys
Logbooks of costly endeavours, captain cooked
by rapacious accountants' conveyance crooks

Yet the grey nomads across the street,
Start to listen to their biorhythms
Caravans' exodus across camel savannah
Unmoored, untethered, lifting anchors
and towbars, travelling the corrugations
the Sahelian shore, Great Sandy deserts

Baobab and spinifex lined Nations
Aboriginal stippled and dotted paintings,
burnt orange ranges and Nullarbor Plains
landscapes. Denuded souls reach, refreshed
No longer extinguished, ready
Untethered, uncoupled for the final journey.

Migratory

I

Suspended between two worlds
One flag flutters one unfurls
Framed by guilt edged bordering

on tightropes walking, vertiginous
Despite the drop, keep your head
Above water at all costs
The current constant unsettling

II

The bird migrates and jettisons
its luggage seeds from the tree
Born in British soil saline tears run deep

Half caste contained in difference
Reduced you're not one of us
In double consciousness

In double complexity we will not retreat
but spread our seed across shallow seas
genetic germinations and generations

stretch boughs back like the hands of clocks
from far away, we sit under shaded limbs
leaves our golden stools and stolen seats

Kings in tree ringed and housed security
Pondering which winged ancestor
carried me? Across the ocean soil
and riverbed, trace the steps, branches
and roots, blue silver threads uncontained
spread their inky messages,
fjord and forge new courses

imagining the ebb and flow
Rooted in one soil, a banyan tree branches out
Flowering other woods whilst its roots ground

deeper, stretching beyond the bordered woodland
across Atlantic seed beds and dark forest floors
Waving v signs high as kites, we migrate and fly.

Wetlands Reverie

Drizzle gently pinpricks my skin
Showering, celestial aspergillum
Clouds burst their ashy canvas sails
in acupuncture rhythms
Burst, time capsules revisioning

Amidst soft sea spray you long
cold needle thudding rain
Fourfold seasoned memories unfurl
the salt cuts deep in pain
Dawn unfolds possibility, to be home again

Eastern grey statues watch
me, deep in thought
in Jurassic aspic frozen,
trapped and caught

Melting into megaflora,
we keep secrets in our pouches
a moment still before we bound off
Journeys to join the dots
on our connected passages
Journeys found and lost

Scar(r)ed Seed

I am scar(r)ed to hold you, as my mother
was scar(r)ed to hold me
I am scar(r)ed to hold myself, I discover
When my seed reaches maturity
Dispersed diaspora seeds
Grey afro blow-outs blown out
Of all proportion, in othered eyes distortion

After the Flood

The billowing mist drifts air eternal
to envelope the diurnal worshipper of gods
and ancestral spirits

A morning thurifer lifts and smokes us
The censer whispers to reveal its secrets
Below reeds bow reverent stems

Bent double dipped in the baptismal font
Water and wine incensed at the altar
The dusky moorhen robed in black cassock,
red frontal shield
and sunset tipped bill

shifts like an ostrich, on the wet mirror ball,
walks like an Egyptian at the local disco
Neck lunging and extending
in staccato stretches

Two cabbage gums stand sentries to my attention
rooted in swampy soil, hovering insects, koalas
and possums chew
its nutrients in blossom eucalypt green-blue

Silky smooth bark blotched and mottled in cream
with khaki chocolate chipped army camouflage
Leaves nascent egg-shaped cabbage await
pregnant in pollen ovulation

Arise the buttercup sun, post flood
unmasking day from dawn
A glinting golden cyclops pierces wattle
Silhouettes, once unshaded seedlings
The cycle path dries up its remnants,
muddy dust of ashes to ashes
seasoning survival messages

Flood ways evaporate and once more
teem with activity
Lined on telegraph wire, cockatoos signal
messages
to complete my living dream.

Healing Tree

For Richie Allen

Hear don't listen, hear the soundwaves of the Rainbow
Serpents' tongues reverberate, through millennia, across iced
land-bridges
Hear don't listen, quench this barren earth
Heal this planet, heal this nation

Tree of shelter, medicine, art, stories, life, Spirituality
Minibeasts burrow in me, squiggle their lines
I'm a weather barometer, moisture reader rooted
In saline soil, my branches manipulated like giant bonsai
Ring trees, ring true, provider of boomerang and digeridoo
Manoeuvre through my sounds, totems and taboos

On the high of Tidbinbilla, a men's sound, a women's sound
Men's business, women's business, planetary business
Ying and Yang, quench this barren earth
Heal this planet, heal this nation

Before me stands proud Kamilaroi/ Ngunnawal man
Lore keeper of the goanna and eagle tip clan
Praising Biami, encouraging me to hear not listen
To the soundwaves, paving millennia-old stories
Hear don't listen, quench this barren earth

Heal this planet, heal this nation.

Family

Personal

Familiar

Watch 'em Grow

Eye watch the pittosporum
s l o w l y   g r o w
Its pale green, grey afro edging over
the gunmetal colorbond fencing
as my kids' limbs, extending, elongating
Buttress roots   beyond
the cloying clay soils of Eastgrove
Make sure you notice

Watch 'em Grow

Uncle & Son

For Oscar Thomas Kofi

His hair curls snail shells, golden, yellow brown
His eyes a green blue Caribbean Sea
Jokes wasteman, mandem innit in merrily
My son a larrikin, a true-blue Aussie
He quakes in rumbles to his Uncle, on the Zoom
Tremors kintsugi gold plating
generations, shaking the room
Genes stitched across silky ocean, kente stripped

How did this come to pass, im augenblick?
My corona prince holds court
vice-taut in linguistic staff grip
A grainy foetus somersaulting flip,
Our hearts gasp... Fufu pounding unfamiliar
vulnerability plays its rhythms
Commanding stories, you own, in laughter peels
From your jolly jumper, you've arisen, majestically!

Soccer Star Floodlights Clouds

For Charlie Yaw Manu

A bullet of energy, a soccer whirling dervish
You rainbow flick the soft IKEA ball in glee
Between the rainclouds of bad moods
Paused on your barometer, mercury at feet
Softly tapping nails upward in keepie-uppie
Outside you hammer it against the wall
Leather on leather, anger dissipating
A ball releasing pent up energy
rebounding molecules and atoms we cannot see

But to see your search to belong so tender
Brown skinned buoy bobbing in white seas
I see a reflection of another
(with tighter coils perhaps but identically)
passing the ball dressed red in Liverpool Hitachi
V-neck and jagged afro – you are me
In happiness and misery.

Cupid's Vinculum

For Ruby Jane Afua

Ruby shuffles down the steps, eyes lit bright
in tandem with Lara, giggling delight
Black lycra gypsy, ballet dress and shoes
Tap dancing laughter lights separating gloom
My sun, my planet, universe my moon
Smooth mischievous criminal, discovering
Beloved hides behind feuding brotherhood
Moon walking lunar landscapes, glowing doom

Yet connects a future that we never knew
How tugs of love break sinews, fibrous
Fractious fractions/ / crack takotsubo pots
The father-daughter-mother/ / / struggling
bitter siblings/ dividing rivalry
////Too many steps to reach Nirvana's dream
Vulgar, unequal denominators
Improper family numerators
Unthinkably split/ /by Cupid's vinculum

Identity Whispers

Identity whispers its name
as mum twists her tongue in labyrinthine Twi
her ring finger encircles the phone cord rosary
umbilical in its myriad divisions and Trinity

Identity etches its name
as dad on his death bed remembers
The Rose & Crown, a Wiltshire lad rounding vowels
at full lilt, eyes twinkle, lips quiver. We tremble

Identity drums its name
as I felt tip Breakdance in brown and pink
lettering, a silky ink nib pressing
on a Kpanlogo antelope skin

Identity calls my name
When Oscar, Charlie and Ruby intone
in Aussie accents, the echo the ring
as broad as the Nullarbor, perfectly at home

Whisper, etch, drum and call
Quench our thirst to its core, offer us Hydration
The many headed gods and goddesses, we implore.

New Australian Wave

Oscar shows me furtively a Snapchat video
on his latest Apple 12 smartphone Pro
Jamie's rapping in a Deep fried gritty Southern drawl
More St. Louis Mississippi Burning cuss words trawl
afloat a muddy hub, drilling trap culture dextrously,
Tap to usurp and sink the gentle flows of the Wollondilly

Far from the deepest darkest Tablelands, Jamie rebrands,
A Cuffay master tailor refashions an accent that
confounds,
to forge diasporan acceptance and belonging, he sounds
out other-brotherly cusses to Bobby in sing song response
the self-improving reflex of a Harlem Renaissance

In testament his scalp's cornrows stretch right back
to parallel times of trickster plantation tactics travel
Conjure and channel Anansi's shapeshifting magically
Score Pele hat-tricks pulling tales out of Brer Rabbits,
skilfully

Three decades before at Cutting Corner, clippers buzzed
I looked in the mirror with a shorn Carl Lewis flat top cut
Dreaming of Jesse Owens and Black Panthers on a podium
I connected Black Atlantic dots across a puzzling odium

Let me return anecdotally, all's not quite what it seems
J's dad hails from small farm Armidale, mum's a Liberian
refugee,
Across the echoing chasm of rippling middle passages
Jamie breaks the chafing chattel chains of slavery
proudly surfing a new Australian wave,
deep in unchartered seize.

Peace After Pain

For Derek Walcott

Love after love as Derek said
and break the bread with your self

In a long conversation
about jealousy and regret
My counsellor reminds me
To love myself

Close my eyes and visualise
A younger carefree version mapped
Red & white hooped socks pulled up
to cover the bitumen scabs

Pastel blue gathered elastic shorts,
a goofy Disney t-shirt
below, a soft side parted afro
snub nose and Bambi eyes aglow

Another me, from a distant
peeled and vulnerable history
I close my eyes in a faithful leap

Disentangling my wounded inner child
I set him free

He's in the room with me, bum high
face on brown carpet lying, I invite him in my lap
Around my arms forever wrapped.

Diaspora³

Diaspora cubed, you can be resigned or fly with it

Diaspora cubed, you can be denied or moved by it

> A paradigm shifts

Twist the multi-colours of the Rubick's

Cubed in superscripted figure 3

> A wholly tripled trinity

Acknowledgements

Grateful acknowledgement is made to the editors of the following anthology, journals and website, in which versions of these poems originally appeared:

An Anthology of Imagined Futures: Poetry for the Planet: "An Ecology of Healing" Edited by Julia Kaylock and Denise O'Hagan, Litoria Press; The Caribbean Writer: "Black Caesarean", "John Randall' and "Underclothed"; Beliveau Review: "South Coast Laurie"; Red Room Poetry: "Healing Tree", shortlisted for Poem Forest.

www.ingramcontent.com/pod-product-compliance
Lightning Source LLC
Chambersburg PA
CBHW051721040426
42446CB00032B/1165